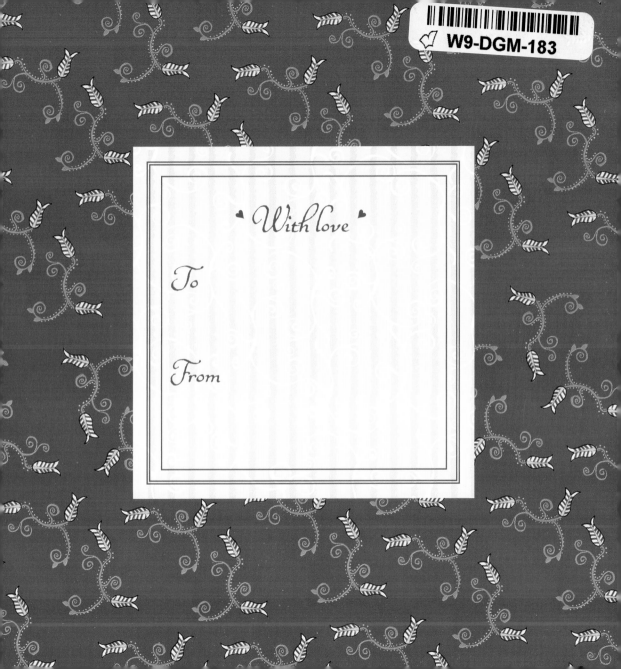

♥ *With love* ♥

To

From

For My Wife

new seasons™

a division of Publications International, Ltd.

new seasons
a division of Publications International, Ltd.

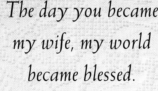

The day you became
my wife, my world
became blessed.

Now join your hands,
and with your hands,
your hearts.

WILLIAM SHAKESPEARE,
KING HENRY THE SIXTH

I am infinitely blessed that in a world full of different people,
you have chosen to give your heart to me.
I am forever grateful that in a world full of different paths,
you have chosen to walk beside me.
I am eternally joyful that in a world full of different opportunities,
you have chosen to create a life with me.

Husband and wife
trust each other with
all their secrets.
They laugh together
and become the
melody and harmony
of a family.

I carry my wife's love
with me always,
like a precious keepsake
clutched to my heart.

The joy of loving you is a blessing beyond compare.
Our lives are a celebration of the special bond we share.

Let my arms be your safe haven,
wrapped around you, strong and warm.
Let my heart be your protector
that will keep you free from harm.
Let love's promise heal your spirit,
bringing everlasting calm.

We may not always be right, but we're always right for each other.
We may not always be perfect, but we're always perfect for one another.
We may not always be happy, but we'll always be happy together.

Marriage is a magical
vehicle in which two distinct
souls journey together to a
shared destination.

The heart that loves is always young.

GREEK PROVERB

The secret to a healthy relationship is for both people to put in more than they take out.

It's easy to love you for all the things we have in common. It's more difficult, but much more valuable, to love the things that set us apart from one another. Learning to appreciate our differences brings a new level of intimacy to our relationship.

*True love is found when
two hearts are going in the same
direction, at a similar pace,
with a compatible outlook.*

With my wife by my side,
I can conquer all the
challenges of life.

Husband and wife are like
marathon runners,
pacing each other
through the race of life.
When one stumbles,
the other drops back to help.
When one surges forward,
the other joins in flight.

Love, like a garden, must be nourished and
cultivated if it is to flourish and thrive.
Take time to pull the weeds, turn the soil,
and plant new seeds. Then enjoy the beauty
of this love we have created.

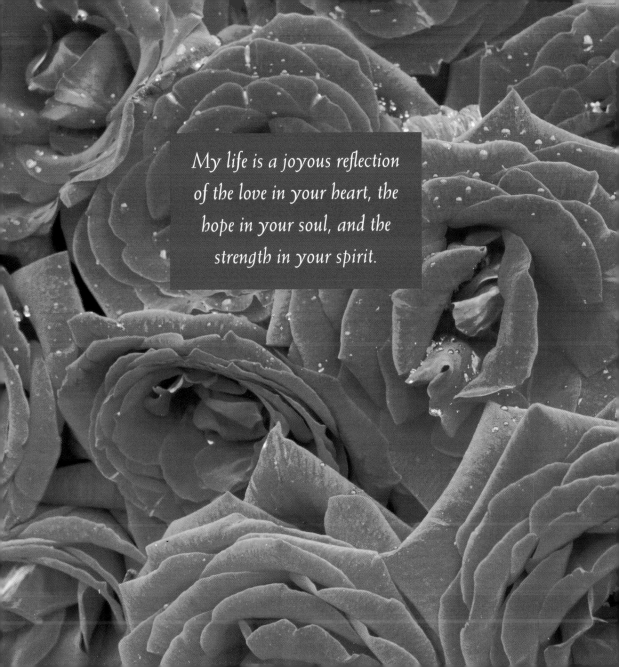

My life is a joyous reflection of the love in your heart, the hope in your soul, and the strength in your spirit.

My wife is a cheerleader when I win,
a counselor when I lose,
a confidante when I need to share,
a clown when I'm feeling blue.

A wife absorbs half your sadness and amplifies twice your joy.

The quality of a marriage
can be measured
by the amount of silence
the two of you are comfortable
letting pass between you
when you are alone together.

When we are truly in love, we see a person's goodness and beauty,
no matter what they look like, how old they are,
what they choose to wear. When we learn to recognize the soul
underneath these outward trappings, our lives are enriched.

Someone to lean on,
someone to laugh with,
someone to share with.
That's what a marriage is.

My wife and I can go anywhere,
do anything together and
have a great time.

Husband and wife share the same vision, but through different sets of eyes.

When I am plodding through my day,
thoroughly immersed in life's present drama,
my wife's love opens my eyes to pleasant events,
happy endings, and hidden treasures.

There are certain things in life on which we can always depend:
The sun will come up tomorrow, the grass will grow,
and true love will flourish.

I cherish my wife as I would cherish my greatest treasure, for that is exactly what she is.

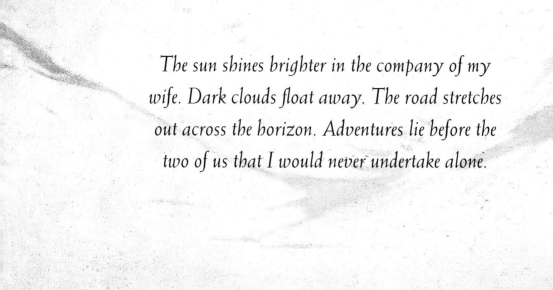

The sun shines brighter in the company of my wife. Dark clouds float away. The road stretches out across the horizon. Adventures lie before the two of us that I would never undertake alone.

Your true love will
never stop
believing in
your dreams.

The path of marriage can take unexpected turns. But it is in its twists and turns, its hills and valleys, that we experience new and surprising joys.

When honesty is tempered with tact, a relationship built on trust is born.

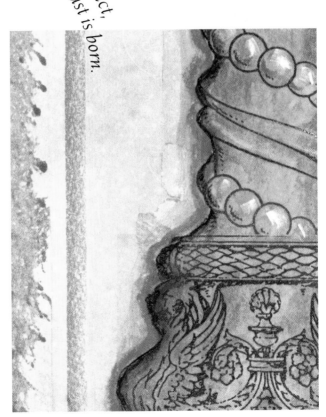

Your happiness means the world to me.
Your smile calls on me to smile.
Your laughter makes me laugh.

A wife is someone who loves and supports you
as you pursue your dreams.

Playing together,
Staying together,
Eating together,
Meeting together,
Living together,
Loving each other.

Devotion—
when bestowed
upon a loving
person—produces
a circle of
wonderful events.

It begins with
returned devotion
and ends with a
mutual desire to
begin the circle
again.

When hearts are melancholy
and souls are feeling blue,
there's nothing like love
to help you make it through.

Sweet memories provide a
comfortable parachute,
allowing us to float through
less-than-perfect moments
and providing a safe landing on
the other side of adversity.

My wife knows that
enough love is never
really enough.

She'll always offer more.

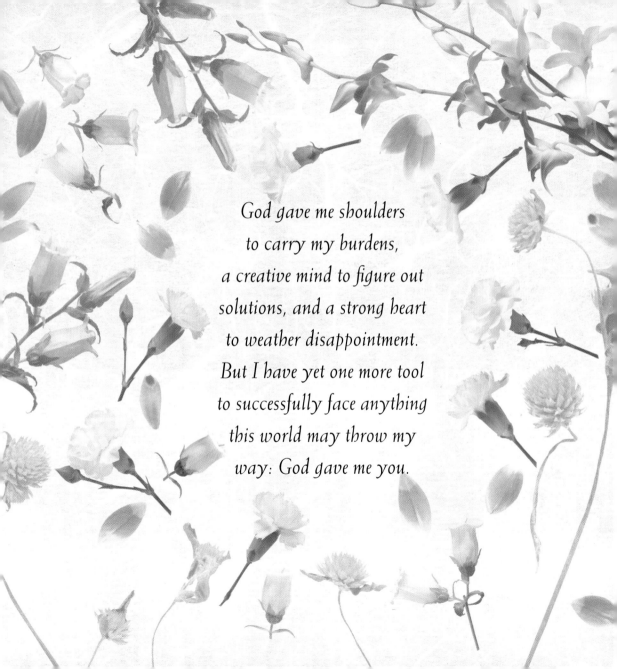

God gave me shoulders
to carry my burdens,
a creative mind to figure out
solutions, and a strong heart
to weather disappointment.
But I have yet one more tool
to successfully face anything
this world may throw my
way: God gave me you.

An honest and true commitment comes from the heart and grows from the soul.

Two souls with but
a single thought,
Two hearts that beat as one.

FRIEDRICH HALM,
DER SOHN DER WILDNESS

springtime of courtship

Like the weather, love has its change of seasons. It begins with the springtime of courtship, merging into the sweet summer of devotion. When autumn arrives, so, too, do the rewards of commitment and sharing.

devotion

Winter often brings a sense of comfort and contentment, but just as the weather is cyclical, so, too, is love. Just beyond the winter is an even brighter spring of renewed passion, internal beauty, and deeper devotion.

If you have something to do,

someone to love,

and something to hope for,

every day becomes a celebration.

The joyous preparation for a marriage begins long before the wedding day is set. It begins when two souls come together, bound by an unseen destiny.

True wealth cannot
be measured in
material objects or
worldly possessions,
but in the depth and
quality of our love.

Love is patient; love is kind; love is not envious or boastful
or arrogant or rude.
It does not insist on its own way; it is not irritable or resentful;
it does not rejoice in wrongdoing, but rejoices in the truth.
It bears all things, believes all things.
hopes all things, endures all things.
Love never ends.

I CORINTHIANS 13:4–8

There is a time in
every relationship
when two people fall
out of a purely
physical attraction.

Theirs is a deeper state
of passion based on
shared values, goals,
and dreams.

This is where real
love begins.

The recipe for a good marriage is equal
parts loving and being loved, giving and
forgiving, caring and being cared for.
It is a constant blending of the ingredients
found within two hearts.

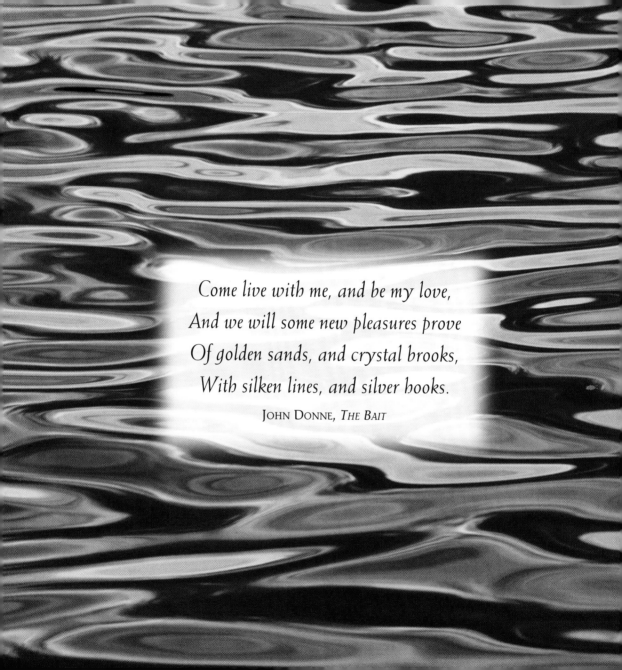

Come live with me, and be my love,
And we will some new pleasures prove
Of golden sands, and crystal brooks,
With silken lines, and silver hooks.

JOHN DONNE, *THE BAIT*

Love makes you complete inside.
A balance is achieved from two
viewpoints, two backgrounds, two hearts.

On our wedding day,
each step down the aisle brought us
closer to the beginning
of a beautiful life together.
Today, we step together,
strolling into our future.

Knowing that I am not alone soothes
my soul and fills my heart.

We shall be one person.

PUEBLO INDIAN

Without you, I am incomplete.
You are my wife, my love.

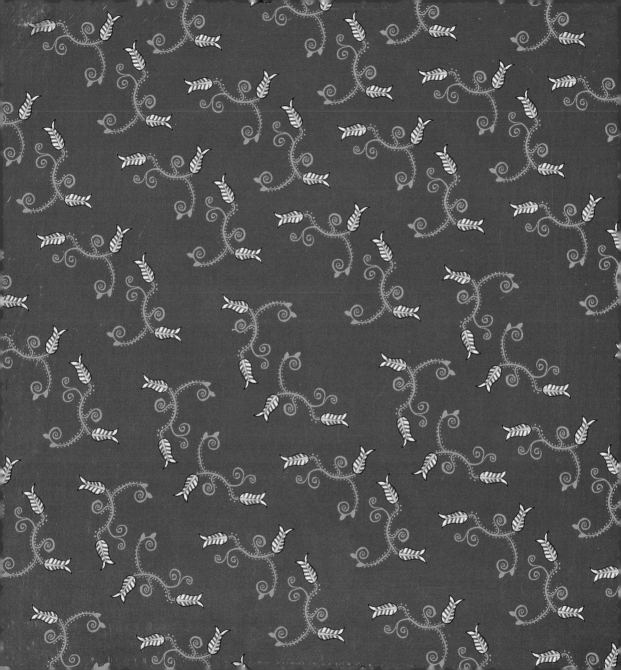